THE ILLUMINATI

Secrets of a New World Order - Conspiracy Theories Book

Phil Coleman

Copyright © 2017.

All rights reserved. No part of this publication may be reproduced, distributed, or transmitted in any form or by any means, including photocopying, recording, or other electronic or mechanical methods, without the prior written permission of the publisher, except in the case of brief quotations embodied in critical reviews and certain other noncommercial uses permitted by copyright law.

This book is intended for informational and entertainment purposes only. The publisher limits all liability arising from this work to the fullest extent of the law.

Table of Contents

Introduction

Part One:

The Rise of the Order

The Fall of the Order

Part Two:

The Three World Wars and the Synagogue of Satan

The Illuminati and Pop Culture

Conclusion

Introduction

The word "Illuminati" has, in recent years, become a catch-all buzzword for conspiracy theories of all sorts. It is a whispered response to strange happenings and seeming coincidences, a screamed retaliation to imbalances of power, a chanting pulse to the unknown.

Beyond this, "Illuminati" has become the punchline of a joke unheard; a sarcastic statement heard around the world--oh, it was the Illuminati, huh? The word has captured the attention of society's collective consciousness in a pervasive manner: but what is it? And how have we come to constantly have it on the tip of our tongues?

"Illuminati" is a word which finds its roots in the Latin plural of the word illuminatus, which means "enlightened." The word itself was adopted by a group of individuals in eighteenth-century Bavaria, known as the Order of Illuminati, but it has since come to mean much more.

With its name now attached to all kinds of secret societies, shadowy projects, and missions to take over the world, it is difficult to separate Illuminati fact from Illuminati fiction. The Illuminati has become a permeating presence whose reality and legends have become intertwined, nearly inseparable on an individual level. As far as whether or not the Illuminati still exists today--well, that's up to you to decide.

Part One:

The Order of Illuminati

Bavarian Roots

Before the Illuminati became the behemoth web of secrets that we think of it today, the group had a humble enough beginning as the Order of Illuminati, also known as the "Bavarian Illuminati" or the "Ancient Illuminated Seers of Bavaria."

Many of the first-hand accounts of this original group were written in German, and it was not until quite recently that any at all were translated into English. For this reason, the Order of Illuminati has been, for hundreds of years, shrouded mostly in mystery for the English-speaking world.

Most of what has been written about the Order of Illuminati relies heavily on information found in the published critiques of John Robison and Augustin Barruel, both of whom had very strong opinions against the original group.

These two accounts, while immensely subjective, are still the most oft-cited sources of information on the Order of Illuminati in the English-speaking world. Both authors quote many accounts of the group's doings, using source documents such as the founder's own accounts and those published by the Bavarian government. However, neither Barruel nor Robison were very diligent in citing their sources, so claims are often made without much context or support.

Overall, our collective knowledge of the original group is truly a working one, comprised mostly of second- and third-hand information and accounts. This being said, the available documents do allow for a fairly comprehensive history of the group's beginnings to be narrativized.

The Order of Illuminati was chartered on May 1, 1776, by a Bavarian citizen named Adam Weishaupt. From the newly translated documents, it is known that the group was originally quite intimate, with only five members' names included in its first charter.

In their original statutes, the group wrote: "The order of the day is to put an end to the machinations of the purveyors of injustice, to control them without dominating them."

Adam Weishaupt was born into a family of professors--both his father and his uncle taught law at the local university. When Adam was five years old, his father died, leaving the boy to be taught by his uncle, who raised Adam with philosophies of the Enlightenment such as rationalism.

Stories of Weishaupt's youth show that he always had a restless mind. He worked his way through his uncle's library in no time flat--a library filled to the brim with French Enlightenment philosophies. These books and his uncle's tutelage brought to

Weishaupt a solid foundation of dislike for the conservative Bavarian ruling class and church.

It was into this tradition of rationalism that Weishaupt founded the Order of Illuminati. Freemasonry was, at the time, becoming increasingly popular in Bavaria and other parts of Europe, but Weishaupt found himself increasingly disillusioned with the Freemason ideals. Weishaupt took it upon himself to form his own group as an alternative--a group whose purpose, as stated in its original documents, was fairly simple: to teach people to be happy by making them good.

And how exactly do you make people good? According to Weishaupt, this could be accomplished by enlightening (by "illuminating") the mind. And, in order to become enlightened, the mind must be completely and utterly free of all prejudice and superstition.

In his original writings, Weishaupt states that his group would create a space free "from all religious prejudices" and that it would cultivate "the social virtues; and animate them by a great, a feasible, and speedy prospect of universal happiness." He proposed that, in order to achieve this, he would create "a state of liberty and moral equality, freed from the obstacles which subordination, rank, and riches, continually throw in our way."

While the Order of Illuminati was founded into a tradition of Enlightenment ideals, its doctrines did make some notable changes to those of other Enlightenment-age thinkers. Immanuel Kant famously stated that a man must make his own way out of immaturity into enlightenment using "his own reason," but the Order of Illuminati prescribed a very detailed list of exactly how its members should try to think, including exactly which works they should read in the attempt to free their minds.

This change in Enlightenment ideals may seem trivial, but it was really quite a departure from Weishaupt's predecessors. Before Weishaupt's Illuminati, the path to true Enlightenment had always been one of the individual.

Weishaupt planned on educating the members of his group using two main principles: that Reason is a supreme power in the world and that one should do unto others as one would like done unto themselves (sometimes known as the Golden Rule). He hoped that, by firmly educating group members using these principles, he would be able to create a domino effect--his students would eventually attain high enough status in society to teach others the same lessons of rationality, and so on. The effects of this movement would, if propagated as hoped, be enormously uplifting to society as a whole.

Weishaupt's character has been questioned time and time again throughout writings on the Order of Illuminati--did his departure (some would say complete dismissal) of key Enlightenment ideals have a nefarious or malicious purpose beyond a turn toward a different sort of illumination? We may never know the answer to this question with any degree of certainty, but it is certainly tragic to think that a man with such good intentions may have become one of the most hated figures of conspiracy thinking.

Based solely off of source documents, Weishaupt's modus operandi for the Illuminati appears to be soundly altruistic (and utopian) in nature, but John Robison and Augustin Barruel, the two authors of English critiques on the Order, immediately saw the group as a radical one, poised in diametric opposition to the church and the Bavarian government.

The Illuminati preached a doctrine of freedom from the church's overbearing domination of philosophy and science in Bavaria, but Robison and Barruel viewed this as a call for the complete destruction of the church as a Bavarian institution. Where Weishaupt pushed forward an agenda of freedom from government oppression, Robison and Barruel understood the group to be working as agents of chaos, yearning for the overwhelming destruction of the government. The Illuminati, in perhaps their most progressive mission, aimed to educate women, but Robison and Barruel saw this as highly unnatural.

In this way, the Order of Illuminati was, from its very inception, a group consistently in doubt by those outside of it. By all hard evidence which exists of the time, naught can be pointed to as an example of the group having secret pining for destruction or the domination of Bavarian society.

Rather, the bare fact of the Order of Illuminati's existence was an affront to those in power, a distinct and loudly heard call for change to the status quo, and this call was not taken well by the general public (or by those in power). The group's inception did take place in the shadows, but those outside the group saw it as much darker than it was to its founder, and vocal critics such as Robison and Barruel made its existence subversive in the public eye.

The Rise of the Order

When the Order of Illuminati first met under the cover of darkness on May 1, 1776, it existed as a petite five-member alliance looking to enact good upon society as a whole.

At this point, the group was still more of a concept than an actuality; a few men took it upon themselves to change the world through enlightenment, and they got together in order to do so. During their first meeting, the five men established the rules which would govern the Order of Illuminati. One of the first of these rules made it clear who would be able to join the Order: all new members of the group must be agreed upon by all existing members and must be well-connected in Bavarian society, with a strong reputation (and a great deal of wealth).

Similarly to the Freemasons, the Order of Illuminati also created a basis of hierarchy within their organization. Upon its first inception, the group had three levels of membership: novices, minervals, and illuminated minervals. "Minerval" refers to the Roman goddess of wisdom, Minerva, as the group hoped to achieve the highest possible levels of illumination and enlightenment in order to change the world.

When the group first began, it was actually known as Bund der Perfektibilisten, which translates roughly to "Covenant of Perfectibility"--it was not until 1778 that the group officially changed its name to

Illuminatenorden (Order of Illuminati), after members began to think that "Covenant of Perfectibility" sounded strange. It is reported that Adam Weishaupt also seriously contemplated using the name "Bee Order" for his group.

The other four members of the original Covenant of Perfectibility were all students of law who studied under Weishaupt at the local University: Massenhausen, Bauhof, Merz and Sutor (the last of whom was later dismissed by Weishaupt for indolence).

Massenhausen was, in the formative years of the Order, the most helpful in expanding the society's membership. Soon after the society's inception, he began to study law in Munich and recruited some new members from the city, including a few of Weishaupt's former pupils who now lived there.

Massenhausen's outreach became one of the Order of Illuminati's largest factors of growth in its early years. However, it is reported that he and Weishaupt did not always agree on this outreach.

Massenhausen began recruiting with, as Weishaupt saw it, an unsavory amount of gusto, reaching out to candidates who did not meet the qualifications set out in the group's original charter. Massenhausen, it seems, longed for the group's expansion into an empire, and he was willing to sacrifice the quality of those in the group if it meant bringing in members who were a bit below the current group's status.

As soon as Weishaupt began to see Massenhausen's recruiting methods as a liability (and, it turns out, his love life had begun to make him neglectful of the group as well), Weishaupt gave control of the new Munich group to a newer recruit, Xavier von Zwack instead. Not long after Zwack's new appointment, Massenhausen (who, it turns out, had also been intercepting mail between Zwack and Weishaupt) graduated, moved outside Bavaria, and completely lost interest in the doings of the order.

Upon his new appointment, Zwack immediately began recruiting for the group using more precise techniques. Christians were most sought after by the group, while pagans, Jews, women, and members of other secret societies were specifically excluded from the Order of Iluminati's recruiting efforts. One would be considered a perfect candidate for the group if one were extremely wealthy, looking to learn, and between the ages of 18 and 30.

By summer's end in 1778, the group had grown in size to be 27 members total, posted in five different locations around the area of Bavaria.

At this point in time, Adam Weishaupt began to find that he was having difficulty in persuading his peers to keep their distance from the Freemasons. The Freemasons, while certainly not a direct rival to the Order, were a large reason as to why Weishaupt had begun his own society in the first place--he found their processes to be far too rigid, leaving almost no room for the introduction of new ideas. This is not to say that Weishaupt's own teachings were not rigid in their own way--remember, after all, that he prescribed a long and specific list of works for his followers to read--but he, at least, believed the Order of Illuminati to be a place tolerant of change and innovation.

However, having found the Freemason's pull to be very seductive to many of those in his social circles, Adam Weishaupt ended up deciding to join the Freemasons in early 1777, in an attempt to glean new material for his own order's rituals. Weishaupt began to make his way through the novice levels of the Freemasons, but he soon found that these entry areas of the order did not really allow him to learn anything at all about the highest parts of the organization, which is what he really yearned to know more about.

In order to gain access to these higher levels of Freemasonry, Zwack suggested that the Order of Illuminati begin negotiating amicable relations with the Freemasons. Frustrated with his attempts thus far to bring any useful information back to his own group, Weishaupt reluctantly agreed, and he soon obtained a permit from a Grand Lodge to open a Freemason lodge called Theodore of the Good Council (in the hope of flattering Charles Theodore, a head of state in Bavaria at the time).

The lodge officially opened its doors in March of 1779, and almost immediately Theodore of the Good Council was packed with members of the Order of Illuminati. By June of the same summer, the lodge's original Master was persuaded to leave, and Weishaupt became the Master of the lodge. It wasn't long until Theodore of the Good Council was recognized widely enough to be considered independent and therefore able to create more lodges as its own. In totality, Weishaupt's side mission into the world of Freemasonry was certainly effective, allowing the Order of Illuminati's influence to spread through the existing networks of the Freemasons.

While the group certainly had humble beginnings, Weishaupt quickly found that he and his allies were not in the minority when it came to aching for change in Bavarian society. By 1982, just six years after the group's first meeting, the Order of Illuminati had grown to include more than 600 members.

As Weishaupt had hoped, this growth was not just random citizens of Bavaria, either-- the group soon drew the attention of some of the highest members of Bavarian society, such as a prominent banker named Mayer Amschel and the Baron Adolph Knigge, both of whom became important funders for the Order during the 1780s.

And, while Weishaupt had initially planned on the group's membership almost exclusively being comprised of his students, by this time the group's reach had expanded to include all kinds of Bavarian citizens: everyone from lawyers to doctors to nobleman had joined the Order of Illuminati by the early 1780s. Several popular writers also joined the group during this time, including Johann Wolfgang von Goethe. By the time 1784 rolled around, the group had picked up nearly 3,000 members.

While Adam Weishaupt was definitely the Order of Illuminati's most influential founder, some of the group's newer recruits also became very influential in its expansion into the 1780s. Baron Knigge, for example, played a very integral role in the Order's evolution as it grew to be a powerful force in Bavarian society.

After joining the group in 1780, Baron Adolph Knigge took a very hands-on approach to his activity in the Order of

Illuminati. At the time, Knigge, only in his early 20s, had already reached some of the highest possible levels in Freemasonry, and he had some very large ideas about how he could reform the group. He had become frustrated with the fact that the Freemasons did not seem at all open to his ideas to change their organization, much as Weishaupt had felt years before.

To this effect, Knigge was pleasantly surprised to hear that a group looking to reform the Freemason ways already existed in the form of the Order of Illuminati.

Knigge was an ideal recruit for the Order of Illuminati because he was extremely well-connected, both within the Freemason community and in the greater Bavarian society as well. Additionally, once he had been shown entry-level papers related to the Illuminati (considered "liberal" by Bavaria and therefore forbidden at the time), he showed continued interest in the group. At this point Weishaupt personally reached out to Knigge, who was flattered by the attention.

Baron Knigge, having reached such high levels of Freemasonry, was very interested in moving quickly through the ranks in the Order of Illuminati, or, at the very least, was hoping to learn details about the higher levels of the organization upon entry. Weishaupt told Knigge that he would need to work toward recruiting new members before he could learn of such secrets, and thusly Knigge's initial role in the organization was just this: a recruiter.

Knigge found himself to be well-suited to this job, although he also found it frustrating to speak to potential new members without knowing at least some details of the higher orders that would await them within the Illuminati. In order to keep Knigge from asking too many questions, Weishaupt gave him the additional job of creating pamphlets about the supposed continued existence of the Jesuits, who had been outlawed many years previously by the Bavarian government. The pamphlets kept him busy for a short while, but he was still troubled by the lack of knowledge he was permitted to have about the Order.

Eventually, he wrote a strongly worded letter to Weishaupt, explaining his discomfort with recruiting new members while not being allowed knowledge of the upper echelons of the Order of Illuminati. Worried that he would soon lose Knigge and his lofty Freemason connections, Weishaupt was forced to admit to the fact that he had fabricated the Illuminati's storied history and had never completed the structure for the highest levels of the organization.

Knigge, who had always hoped to create an improved version of the Freemasonic organization, took this surprise in stride. He told Weishaupt not to worry about it--he would help to finish writing the structure of the Order of Illuminati up to the highest level, using his working knowledge of Freemasonry.

By 1982, Knigge had written a full re-working of the Order's ranking system. The revised version of this system had three classes, which were then further split into subdivisions such as "Novicate" and "Apprentice," as well as the higher classes of "Prince," "Mage," and "King," although historians agree that the full rituals for these higher classes were never completed by Knigge and Weishaupt.

Knigge also believed that the Order of Illuminati could benefit from some of the other rites of passage used in the Freemasons. He suggested that each new member be given a secret classical name, as was a tradition of Freemasonry. For example, Knigge was known amongst his peers as Philo, Weishaupt as Spartacus.

In the years following Knigge's acceptance into the Order, the organization grew more than it ever had before. The Order's efforts to recruit through Freemason channels worked to a certain extent, although often not exactly to the extent which Weishaupt would have hoped. Knigge targeted specific lodge masters who he believed would be interested in the Order of Illuminati's mission, and, once or twice, this worked, and entire masonic lodges were essentially converted to the Illuminati cause.

However, the Freemasons, as he already knew, were mostly very set in their ways, and thus even making use of their extensive networks proved difficult. Even with sound reasoning, it is difficult to persuade a stubborn network of people to join a reformed (but similar) organization. Most of the Order's recruiting efforts through existing Freemason networks were met with failure. Even those who saw the Illuminati as a possible ally against common forces of evil enjoyed their freedom in independent Freemason lodges far too much to join another closed society.

During the first half of 1780s, the Order of Illuminati was able to bring in high-ranking recruits, simultaneously boosting their reputation in the community and continuously opening up new networking pathways for further recruiting. The group also spread its influence geographically, opening additional posts both within and outside of Bavaria. The group which had from its small-time beginnings hoped to change the world for good may not have accomplished this goal quite yet--but it was certainly finding many others who hoped to do the same, in the process greatly increasing the chances of reaching their collective altruistic goals.

The Fall of the Order

No matter what is known or said about the Order of Illuminati, it is difficult to deny the beauty with which it spread throughout Bavaria and the surrounding area in the years following its original charter.

By all first-hand accounts, Adam Weishaupt set out to create a space for his peers and students to meet as a force for good. The Order of Illuminati grew out of a tradition older than we can trace through the written record--a tradition of coming together for a common cause, of wanting to move forward, a tradition which, time and time again, has hoped to tilt the planet's spin in just precisely the right direction to maximize our progress toward something better.

The Order of Illuminati--which had begun as just one man and his four students--numbered almost 3,000 men by the conclusion of 1784. In just eight years, the Order of Illuminati grew to be nearly 600 times its original size.

By early 1783, the Order had almost completely given up on its efforts to recruit through Freemason channels, but this certainly did not stop them from moving forward with the kind of recruiting which had gotten them to where they were in the first place. Individual recruiting continued, at an even faster pace than ever before.

Around this time, the government of Bavaria was going through relatively significant changes, shifting the entire atmosphere of

Bavarian society ever so slightly. The succession of Charles Theodore (the very man to whom the Illuminati had dedicated their Freemason Lodge) to the Bavarian position of Elector led to a rise in liberal attitudes in Bavaria, something the Order of Illuminati had hoped for since its first days as an organization.

Charles Theodore, an oft-criticized leader of Bavaria, cared deeply about arts and philosophy, and never thought much of politics. He liked to think of himself as a Prince of Peace, much unlike others who had held his position before him. While the Order was vocally against the Bavarian government's old-fashioned conservatism, the succession of Charles Theodore to the Elector seat was, to the Order, a step in the right direction--that is, at least in the beginning.

While he was much more liberal than his predecessors, Charles Theodore was also, it is reported, kind of a pushover. His disregard for politics turned out to be less of an asset than the Illuminati had hoped, and, soon after his succession as Elector of Bavaria, other noblemen and the clergy soon persuaded him to revert the country back to its former state of repressed liberal thinking.

Progress, it seems, would have been detrimental to those in power, and thusly they hoped to instead maintain the status quo. Charles Theodore, a man who couldn't care less which way the country's government leaned, turned out to be the perfect man to help the country tread its conservative waters. Conservative thinking soon became the law of the land once again.

Despite his weak-willed nature and his government's penchant for repressing liberal thought, Charles Theodore actually helped the Illuminati's recruiting efforts. The quick respite from the overbearing conservativity of Bavaria was a breath of fresh air to educated thinkers of the late 18th century, and the very quick return to conservatism greatly angered the educated of Bavaria. The Order of Illuminati took advantage of this disappointment by offering a place for these educated thinkers to join others in their dissent. The number of members grew exponentially in 1783, and the Illuminati expanded its reach ever further into Europe.

Illuminati posts soon opened in Warsaw, Austria, and even Switzerland.

The exact number of members in the Order by this time was claimed by Weishaupt to reach nearly 3,000, although the group's charters only name 650 individuals who had signed their names in allegiance to the Illuminati. It is estimated that many others existed without stating such as official members, and that even more took part in the Order as members of Illuminati-owned Freemason lodges.

No matter the exact number of members, it should not be downplayed just how influential the Order of Illuminati became by 1784. The organization was by no means a majority within Bavarian society, but it had intertwined very intimately with all manner of high-standing individuals. The Order still had its basis of members who were doctors, lawyers, and academics, but it had also grown to include governors, chancellors, ambassadors, Dukes, and even the minister of public education. The Order had grown into a thriving, twining organization, with its feet planted firmly all around Bavaria and the surrounding area.

This is not to say, of course, that the Illuminati now existed without critical peers. Several prominent authors of the time took a less romantic view of the Order of Illuminati; some criticized the ever-persistent "secret" nature of the organization, while others poked fun at its seemingly altruistic goals. If membership was so important that the Order dedicated most of its time to recruiting efforts, how would they ever accomplish anything?

The larger the Order of Illuminati grew, the more opportunities it opened itself up for dissent and disappointment. And thus, while 1783 and 1784 ended up being some of the organization's most lucrative years for membership, they were also the most difficult for the blossoming group to navigate.

During the early 1780s, the Bavarian government did not seem overly concerned with the Order of Illuminati in particular (although they did continue their war on anything that got too close to liberalism). Rather, the Order's most notable conflicts were from other groups with similar missions to the Illuminati's. While it would be pleasant to imagine a world where forces of progress unite together under a common goal to fight the forces of evil and create a more tolerant society of do-gooders, it turns out this may have been just a bit too utopian for 18th century Bavaria.

One of the main reasons Adam Weishaupt continued to keep the Order of Illuminati a secret was because of his opposition: the Freemasons. The Freemason society, while often running parallel to the Illuminati in their concerns for enacting good upon the world, were, for the most part, not very accepting of the Order.

The main opposition to the Illuminati was the pull of Rosicrucianism, a mystic order which had taken over a large amount of real estate in the German Freemason society. The Rosicrucians were a cultural group which grew popular in the 17th and 18th centuries, claiming to have insider knowledge into a doctrine about the order of the world built on truths from the ancient past. What remains of the manifesto of the Rosicrucians seems to point to it being comprised of a combination of disciplines including Kabbalah and Christianity.

Like the Order of Illuminati, the Rosicrucians reported that their goal was a complete reformation of mankind toward the powers of good through the use of enlightenment. However, their use of religious artifacts, lore, and their reported mystical rituals (which seem to be closer to seances than anything else) made the Rosicrucians differ in extremely important ways from the Illuminati.

Adam Weishaupt was wary of the Rosicrucians and the hold they had on the German Freemasons. He, too, was aware of the similarities between his own organization and theirs, but the Rosicrucians' actions were antithetical to the Illuminati's call for a rationalist state in Bavaria. In order to avoid mounting tensions between the groups, Weishaupt continued to keep the Order of Illuminati as secret as possible. In this way, the Illuminati, a group which had always existed on the fringes of Bavarian society, burrowed further underground (or, at least, as far underground as they could go while still recruiting new members).

This effort turned out to be futile. Adolph Knigge had already attempted to recruit a few high-ranking Freemasons with Rosicrucian sympathies, and, soon, the Rosicrucians began to attack the Order of Illuminati directly and without sympathy. Through the use of Freemason lodges under their control, the Rosicrucians began to spread messages against the Illuminati, calling them revolutionaries and atheists.

For the Order of Illuminati, this negative press was incredibly harmful. The Rosicrucians began to warn all Freemasons against the Order, claiming to have read "appalling documents" by the Order which called for the demise of all religious groups. These verbal attacks lasted over a year, culminating in a decree that any men who had declared their allegiance to the Illuminati would no longer be allowed to be initiated as a Freemason.

The Rosicrucians also reportedly spied on high-level members of the Illuminati during this time. Their attacks completely ended recruiting efforts by the Illuminati in many areas of Germany.

In this way, the Rosicrucians--a group which, at least in their end-goals, was very similar to the Order--did quite a deal of damage to the Illuminati, in current membership, recruiting efforts, and, maybe most importantly, in reputation. The Order had become large enough by 1784 to warrant very real enemies for the group in Bavarian society. The purpose of the Order of Illuminati had always been to work beneath the surface of society to make change for the better, but the conflict with the Rosicrucians made the group much more known (and known as a dangerous group, at that).

And thus we reach the peak of the Illuminati's time in Bavaria--nearly 3,000 members strong, by Weishaupt's count, and, up so high for all to see, it would not take much more than a strong wind to begin a mighty fall.

Around the time of the Rosicrucian attacks, the Order of Illuminati found themselves with discontent within their own organization as well. Some of the highest-ranking council members within the Order argued with Weishaupt over the minutiae of the organization's proceedings (including, but certainly not limited to, recruiting efforts). Weishaupt argued right back, writing more than one strongly worded letter about the dissenting Illuminati, complaining about them to others within the group whom he perceived to be allies.

More important to note about the state of the Order of Illuminati during this time was Weishaupt's quickly fraying relationship with Adolph Knigge. Knigge, who had first entered the Order in 1780, eager to learn about the organization and bring lessons from Freemasonry to improve it, would barely be taking part in the Illuminati just four years later.

When Knigge first joined the Illuminati, Weishaupt gave him free reign to essentially write and re-write any parts of the Illuminati rituals which he thought could benefit from Freemasonry's own rites and organizing principles. By 1784, however, Weishaupt felt Knigge may have actually been given too much power in this. Weishaupt, by 1784, was no longer interested in allowing Knigge to exercise this level of power over the Order and what it would evolve into in the future.

At the same time, Knigge felt that his role in the organization's rise had actually been downplayed, and that he deserved more credit than he was being given for the state of the Order as it came to be. Weishaupt brought the society into being with his reformed Enlightenment ideals and his quest for a better tomorrow, but Knigge had elevated what started as not much more than a glorified club into the wide-reaching organization it had become.

Weishaupt and Knigge had disagreed on ideological grounds from the first day of their partnership--Knigge leaned much more toward the mystic side of the Illuminati, while Weishaupt, true to his upbringing and his tutelage, consistently aired more on the side of rationality--and this conflict of interests, too, began to boil over in 1784.

The two composed the rites and rituals for the status of Priest together, one of the highest in the Order of Illuminati, and other high-ranking members of the Order were vocally against the rituals, saying they were overly complicated and ridiculously expensive to uphold.

Upon hearing of just how much discontent was brewing in the group because of the new rituals, Weishaupt quickly ordered Knigge to re-write and re-circulate them. The issue at hand was this: the papers stating the rituals and regalia of the Priest order had already been posted. As with all of the Illuminati's rituals, Weishaupt had passed them off as having ancient origins (despite having only been written quite recently).

However, Weishaupt seemed not to care much about this mammoth-sized inconsistency in his preaching--rather than leaving the Priest rituals as they were, doing his best to keep the image of the ancient rituals intact, he began bad-mouthing Knigge by telling other Order members that it was Knigge's fault the ritual had been written so poorly.

Knigge, for his own part, did not take kindly to this. He threatened Weishaupt, stating that, if the slander against him continued, he would reveal to the Illuminati just how much of the documentation for the organization had been written by him.

It is important to note here that, while both Knigge and Weishaupt obviously had reason to be angry at the other party, it was the base lie of the Order of Illuminati which truly tore them apart--the lie that the Illuminati and all of its organizing principles had been passed down since ancient times. The Order was of course a secret society, but Weishaupt and Knigge built a small, rationalistic empire on a fabrication. From its founding, the Order of Illuminati sat on a bed of lies, and this foundation began to crack under the pressure of its dueling creators.

Knigge attempted to sabotage the Order of Illuminati from the inside, but this turned to failure, as most who he attempted to bring on board with his rebellion trusted Weishaupt too deeply for any measurable sort of betrayal.

By the end of the summer of 1784, Adolph Knigge had completely removed himself from the Order of Illuminati. He and Weishaupt came to an agreement whereby Knigge would return all of his Illuminati documents to Weishaupt. In return, Weishaupt would publicly retract all negative comments he had made against Knigge.

While this agreement points to a degree of civility to the ending of the disputes between Knigge and Weishaupt, Knigge's removal from the organization was detrimental to the progress it had made. Despite the shortcomings Weishaupt saw in him, Baron Knigge was by far the best recruiter and theoretician that the Illuminati had at their disposal. Without him (and his ties to Freemasonry), the group would have had a great deal more difficulty in growing to even a fraction of the formidable organization it eventually became.

Once Knigge left the Order, it wasn't long until the whole operation came crumbling down around itself.

Besides having conflicts of identity within its ranks, the Order of Illuminati had, in the 1780s, become a society which put its recruiting efforts as top priority on its to-do list. The valiant causes preached by Adam Weishaupt to his four students in early May of 1776 took the backburner to causes of membership and growth. The Illuminati, by its end, was still thinking in terms of lofty societal changes, but its methods to do so had altered--it had become a game of power and numbers.

Secret societies may operate in full daylight, but they still move in whispers, sticking to the shade, hoping to keep their intricacies under wraps to those outside of the organization. Secret societies are, most of the time, about secrets, not about being large and far-reaching, and this is where the Order of Illuminati began to differ from other secret societies.

3,000 members is a very large amount of people, and, no matter how well you attempt swear them to secrecy, there is always a chance that one (or a few of them) will do a sub-par job of keeping quiet.

Tragically enough, this is exactly where the Order of Illuminati found their downfall. Low-ranking members of the Illuminati began to brag about the group's power, speaking about the Order as a serious threat to the German monarchy (and to the monarchical government system as a whole). Despite higher-ranking officials' attempts to slow this sort of braggery, it is reported that these members also spoke freely and publicly about important members of the Order, in attempts to show to others just how much the Illuminati were a force to be reckoned with.

By the end of 1784, the existence of the Order of Illuminati had essentially become public knowledge. This is not to say that a great deal of the actual happenings within the organization was not still kept a secret--because they largely were--but the Order of Illuminati itself was no longer a secret. The whispers on the street were no longer Illuminati members planning their next meetings: the whispers were non-Illuminati wondering to each other whether or not they could trust their public figures, now that they knew what they were up to in their free time. Many members of the Illuminati held power in Bavarian society, a fact which was not taken lightly by their constituents.

The fact that the Order of Illuminati began and operated in secret began to work against the group. The public questioned this secretive nature--what was the organization's true purpose? If it had worked so hard to stay hidden, did it have more nefarious goals than simple societal reform? Soon the Illuminati had all sorts of things blamed on them, including a few particularly radical anti-religious pamphlets which were circulating Bavaria at the time.

One complaint by the Bavarian public was that those in the Order of Illuminati were being given special treatment in legal matters. To be fair, this particular complaint had a degree of truth to it--Illuminati members did hold positions in high courts, and reports show that these officials did give their fellow Illuminati members more mellow sentences than they did to the general public.

The murmured hum of disquiet at the Order of Illuminati's public reveal soon turned to a buzz, and then an out roar, and Charles Theodore took it upon himself to end the business once and for all. On March 2, 1785,

Theodore submitted a government edict to the public which banned all secret societies from Bavaria. By the time the edict had been posted, Adam Weishaupt had already fled Bavaria. Documents and correspondence pertaining to the Order of Illuminati were published by the government in 1787.

The Order of Illuminati dispersed quickly and quietly, leaving behind nothing lasting of their mission for good.

Part Two:

Modern Illuminati Secrets

The New World Order

The Order of Illuminati was officially disbanded in 1785 with the government-issued edict declaring an end to all secret societies in Bavaria, but this does not necessarily mean the group ceased to exist in other forms.

From its first days as an organization, the Illuminati worked in the shadows of society. While their activities eventually came to light through the publication of their official documents and correspondence, the details of such did manage to stay a secret for quite some time. Even with this publication, there is no way of knowing that Adam Weishaupt did not take some Illuminati materials with him when he fled Bavaria.

Beyond this, there is no telling what happened to all 3,000 members of the Order of Illuminati after it had been outlawed. The organization had existed near the boundaries of the law since 1776--who is to say it didn't continue as such after it had officially disbanded? Maybe--just maybe--its members continued to meet in the dead of night, in basements and in deserted churches, whispering collective knowledge by candlelight.

The Order of Illuminati's reach had become fairly invasive in Bavarian society by 1785, and it is difficult to believe that, at the snap of one elector's fingers, its membership would collectively give up on the mission for which they had worked so hard.

We have no way of knowing where the influence of the Order of Illuminati extended, after it disbanded, because any official documentation of the group ended in 1785. From there on out, it is all speculation.

As mentioned earlier in this book, the Order of Illuminati was used as a scapegoat for theories of conspiracies before it had even gone dark. Once word got out that a secret society had been operating in Bavaria for close to a decade, both the government and the public decided that said society had the potential to have had a hand in any and every misfortune or act of rebellion that had taken place in Bavaria since its inception.

The rest of the world learned about the Order of Illuminati not too long after it was outlawed, but the information which escaped Bavaria was scant and incredibly biased. The original documents found and published by the government were only ever made available (until quite recently) in the original German, and thus the only ways in which the English-speaking world was able to make any sense of the Illuminati business was through third-party writings and critiques on the matter.

The two main sources of information on the Order of Illuminati for the English-speaking world were two critiques, published by

Augustin Barruel and John Robison. Both works were highly critical of the Order and, more importantly, were highly skeptical of its self-professed and altruistic goals. To this effect, both Barruel and Robison wrote what claimed to be "histories" of the Order but ended up being no more than long, ranting, scathing reviews of the organization.

Robison and Barruel's narratives about the Order of Illuminati are each colored by their authors' dislike for the mission of the organization--both disagreed with what the Illuminati set out to do, and thusly their accounts of the organization do not tell very objective tales. Robison's piece in particular did not even try to hide the fact that it was extremely subjective--its title was Proofs of a Conspiracy--and he goes as far as to suggest that the Order of Illuminati was pulling strings which somehow led to the French Revolution.

News of the Order and its downfall swiftly and surely made its way over Europe, across the Atlantic Ocean, and into the newly independent United States of America. As Robison and Barruel's publications were the only ones made available in English at the time, these accounts was the only way for Americans to understand what had happened with the group. Leaders of the American colonies (including, but certainly not limited to, clergymen) began to preach against the evils of the Illuminati. Newspapers printed articles about the Order's great and terrible power.

This hysteria did not last long, and the majority of the world's concern for the Order of Illuminati's secret handiwork died down in the early part of the 19th century, although it did, from time to time, get brought up again.

But the world has not completely forgotten. Ever since the group officially disbanded in 1785, the word "Illuminati" has been a whisper on the lips of the world. The society began in secret, and it existed most of its lifespan in secret, so who is to say exactly what went on at Illuminati meetings, behind closed doors? And who is to say that the Illuminati every truly disbanded?

As with many secrets, the world wondered, kept wondering--and is still wondering, to this day. The Illuminati left Bavaria in 1785 with a trail of whispers behind them, and this trail still exists today. The society existed within a veil of society's doubt for their "true" goals--from its creation; the group was treated as if it was hoping to overthrow the government.

Many have never stopped their wonderings about what really happened to the Order of Illuminati after it had disbanded. This has resulted in a wide variety of theories being attached to the group's name. Many of these theories leave loose threads and, and even more of them are brief, without any sort of substantial evidence to back them up--but there are also many commonalities between these theories, a loose joining of narratives which creates a semi-cohesive whole, painting a picture (albeit a relatively abstract one) of what the Illuminati may be up to today.

Many of those who theorize about the Illuminati's doings in modern society are labeled as crazy or crackpots. Their theories are called conspiracies because there is no hard evidence to back them up. In other circumstances, believing in higher levels of organization without hard evidence is called faith.

There is no way that one can prove the validity of narratives told about the Illuminati, but there is also no concrete evidence to disprove these theories. And thus they are just that--theories.

In order to understand the Zeitgeist around the Illuminati today, one must first delve into the theory of the New World Order. While accounts of the New World Order vary as they are told and retold by a myriad of theorists, there are some important parts of the theory which are integral to any understanding of it.

The New World order is, at its base level, a top-secret group of elites who are attempting to take over the world. The term "New World Order" was first used by multiple government leaders in the early 20th century to describe an era of unprecedented change in the world, brought on by the events of World War I and World War II. These leaders believed the global scale of these events vastly changed the scope of political thinking and allowed for worldwide reform. There was a sense in the air that countries could come together to enact good in the world, rather than simply existing as independent entities.

This rising feeling of global potential for change led to the creation of organizations such as the North Atlantic Treaty Organization (NATO) and the United Nations (UN), both of whom hoped to create spaces of global-level thinking which had not previously existed. These progressive organizations were welcomed by many around the world, although some did not believe in their ability to enact good and took it upon themselves to create other movements with similar goals.

During the 1940s, authors such as H.G. Wells began to use their writings to expand thought on the idea of a "new world order." Ideas such as a globally planned economy and a class of global overlords became popular around this time, more as fodder for thought than anything else, but it wasn't long before these ideas took a menacing turn in the eyes of the general public.

The Red Scare of the 1940s and 1950s created a culture of conspiracy and questioning in the United States. While the Red Scare primarily focused its hysteria on the un-American spread of communism in the United States, it had the unintended side effect of making a norm out of conspiracies. No longer was a neighbor simply a neighbor--now that neighbor had the very real potential of hiding something from you; that very neighbor for whom you once baked cookies may very well be working as a spy for the Soviet Union.

This culture of distrust may have begun at a governmental level (with, for example, the House of Un-American Activities Committee), but it soon trickled down into the general public as well. It was not uncommon to turn friends and former allies in for suspicion of communist sensibilities. Anyone and everyone could be spreading communism throughout America--there was just no way to know, not anymore.

For this reason, the middle of the 20th century was a time of both peace and of unrest with this peace in the United States.

During this time, it also became very popular to publish theories on what exactly was being hidden in plain sight. The Red Scare became a time during which it was completely acceptable (and, even, encouraged) to blame the woes of the world upon a larger conspiracy.

In the United States, the political right in particular found solace in demonizing their opponents in this way. Conservative citizens began to theorize that most liberal political agendas--including but not limited to welfare and international aid--were part of a large-scale plot to spread communism and completely replace individual nations with one global communist government (the supposed New World Order).

The later part of the Cold War did nothing to help these conspiratorial sensibilities in the United States, as during this period, tensions with the spread of communism and the threat of a nuclear apocalypse were at an all-time high. Destruction was just around every corner, if you knew where to look for it, and thusly there was almost always something lying in wait in the shadows. What exactly it was that was waiting was up to much discussion, and conspiracy theories grew naturally from this gap in knowledge.

While they may not always be mentioned in the discussion of the New World Order, the Illuminati never fully faded from the American horizon. As mentioned earlier in this book, the Illuminati were connected to conspiracy theories almost from the time of the group's first charter, and, in particular, toward the end of said charter, when the group was no longer much of a secret. The Order of Illuminati was disbanded, after all, because Charles Theodor of Bavaria believed the group was hoping to overthrow the monarchy and destroy Roman Catholicism.

John Robison and Augustin Barruel also each had heavy hands in the Illuminati's growth to a conspiracy phenomenon. Both believed (and published information stating such) that the Order of Illuminati actually hoped to bring about a wave of revolutionary thinking in Europe during the late 18th and early 19th centuries. The Illuminati, in this way, became a figurehead for the spread of movements against the monarchical system of government, the patriarchy, and, ultimately, as agents of chaos.

The mass publication of these claims led to a great deal of hysteria in Europe during the 19th century, especially in noblemen and other rulers of the time. And, in fact, many leaders took preventative action against secret societies such as the Illuminati by enforcing even more conservative and oppressive laws in their territories, spawning the very sort of revolutions they had originally hoped to prevent.

More recently, theorists have published arguments stating that Jewish elites are actually the heads of the Illuminati, serving both the spread of capitalism and communism. Nesta Helen Webster, for example, posited that the reason both were being spread was in order to divide the world and then conquer it. Many evangelists and followers of fundamental Christianity became the main source of the spread of Illuminati-fueled conspiracy theories well into the 20th century.

The New World Order is important to an understanding of the Illuminati because it is the thread which ties together a great deal of pervasive conspiracy theories. It is the answer to the question which follows the seeds of a conspiracy to the grave--it is the "so what?" of conspiracy theories. So the Illuminati still exist and are operating today--but why? The New World Order answers this question by positing that the Illuminati are now seeking to rule the entire planet with a single government entity. The theory also links the Illuminati to many other secret societies and conspiracy theories, such as those which exist around the Freemasons and End Time (an apocalyptic conspiracy theory).

While conspiracies around the New World Order began as stories told by theorists to dark rooms with a few people willing to listen, they have grown to be a worldwide phenomenon. Hollywood picked up the conspiracy theory bug in the 1990s, and television and movies soon began to reflect the values of conspiracy theories as well. One notable example of the popularization of conspiracy theories is The X-Files, a show which spanned nearly a decade of television and introduced millions of viewers to the idea of complex, worldwide conspiracies.

Political scientists have worried, in recent years that the rise of conspiracy theories in popular culture--especially the New World Order, a theory whose scale is unprecedented--could have very tangible, real-world effects on terrorism and authoritarian power sources around the world.

While the Illuminati's role in the New World Order is not often discussed beyond simply calling them the puppet masters of the entire operation, it is nonetheless important to note that the Illuminati do play this important role in one of the largest-scale theories published thus far.

The Three World Wars and the Synagogue of Satan

One author in particular, William Guy Carr, was extremely influential in this period's understanding of conspiracy theories. William Carr, by all accounts, led a simple life; born in England, he was educated in Scotland, and by the time he was fourteen years old, he went to sea. He served in the navy in both World War I and World War II, and he spent most of his naval career in different areas of Canada (mostly Newfoundland and Nova Scotia).

By the time the 1930s rolled around, William Carr was holding talks at clubs around Canada, claiming to have gleaned insider knowledge about what he called "international conspiracies." To Carr, these conspiracies were divided into "international communism" and "international capitalism."

William Carr believed the Illuminati were largely responsible for both of these conspiracies--he called them the "international bankers," and believed that the Rothschild and Rockefeller families controlled a large majority of these bankers. Carr supposedly drew much of this theory from his experience in the navy during World War I, but he also cites Augustin Barruel and John Robison as sources for his information on the Illuminati.

While Carr's theories were originally very thin, underdeveloped, and mutable, by the end of World War II he began to publish more impressively fleshed-out theories of world domination.

In order for Carr's theories to make historical sense, he first must establish a narrative of what exactly happened to the Illuminati after their official disbandment in 1785. William Carr's answer to this question is succinct: the Order of Illuminati went underground. The group had already dug their roots into the Freemason network as it existed in Bavaria, Germany, and Switzerland--Carr suggests that Adam Weishaupt instructed Illuminati members to further infiltrate Freemason lodges after secret societies were outlawed. In this way, the Illuminati actually became a secret society within a secret society.

Much of Carr's reasoning as to what happened to the Illuminati after the royal edict in 1785 is actually based in John Robison's publication from 1798. Robison claims to have been invited to join the Illuminati in Britain not long after the group had officially closed their doors, in an attempt to bring the Illuminati to England. Robison stated that, within Freemason channels, only members who had proved themselves as "defected from God" and interested in the international sphere were inducted into the Illuminati.

Robison claims to have been given a copy of Adam Weishaupt's "Revised Conspiracy" for safekeeping, as he kept his opinions to himself on the matter. Robison published his own thoughts on the Illuminati in 1798 as a warning to heads of clergy and government about the power of the Illuminati. Carr believes his warnings were largely ignored because of the very power which the Illuminati wielded within government and church organizations, allowing them to dampen the effects of the warnings.

By using Robison as his base source (his text was, after all, one of the only ones readily available in English); Carr posited that the Illuminati had never truly disbanded--they had simply burrowed further underground, using the Freemason network to their advantage.

It is impossible to tell exactly how much of Robison's account is true and how much is fabricated--he was really very liberal with citing his sources, and spent most of his time waxing poetic about the impending revolution rather than actually picking his facts wisely. No matter its shortcomings, Robison's account is important here in that it spawned so many other popular conspiracies involving the Illuminati.

In his book Pawns in the Game, William Guy Carr outlines one of his most pervasive theories regarding exactly what the Illuminati have been up to since being outlawed, which he calls the "Three World Wars" (sometimes known as the 3WW).

In this book, Carr theorizes that World War I boiled down to one ultimate goal: the Illuminati hoping to overthrow the Russian Tsars and turn Russia into the effective center of a worldwide strain of communism. According to Carr, the British Empire and the German Empire were stirred to action by the Illuminati, who hoped to use existing conflicts between the two countries as a provocation point for the war.

After the conclusion of World War I, Carr theorizes, the Illuminati used communism to overthrow existing power structures and weaken the hold religion had on the world at the time. Afterward, World War II was brought to life by using existing conflicts between fascists and political Zionists. Essentially, Carr argues that all of World War II was fought so that Nazism could be squashed and the state of Israel could be created in Palestine.

During World War II, Carr states, communism was meant to be able to build itself up internationally to the point where it would rival Christianity in the hold it held over the world. At this point, the power of communism would be held in place until it needed to be used for further cataclysm in the future.

Pawns in the Game was published in 1955, and, while most of the book revolves around secrets of events which took place in the past, William Carr also takes time to speak about how exactly the Illuminati plan on using the Three World Wars to their advantage in the future.

Carr states in his work that he possesses a copy of a speech made in 1952 by a rabbi named Emanuel Rabinovich, in which it is supposedly stated that the Illuminati hope to bring World War III into being within five years. During this war, many smaller countries would side with either Russia or the United States, while Israel would remain largely neutral. This particular war would be stirred up by the differences found between the political Zionists and the leaders of the Muslim world.

After World War Three, Carr warns, the nihilists and the atheists will yearn for world domination more than ever before, leading to a social cataclysm the likes of which has never before been seen. Eventually, he says, the Illuminati plan for this cataclysm to completely end religion, wiping out the "white race" along with it. He suggests that the best way to combat the Illuminati's plan for ultimate chaos and world domination is to "support Christianity against all forms of atheism and secularism."

Another of William Carr's most important and lasting theories involving the Illuminati is termed the "Synagogue of Satan," originally referred to by Carr as the "World Revolutionary Movement." While the word synagogue brings with it Judaic connotations, Carr made it clear in his writings that he does not believe the Synagogue of Satan is Jewish.

Carr's Synagogue of Satan is, at a basic level, just what it sounds like: a satanic cult. Carr used a biblical verse as the basis of his argument, essentially stating that the

Synagogue of Satan would be comprised of people who claim to follow Judaic traditions but who really only use this religion as a cover for their satanic rituals.

William Carr's theory of the Synagogue of Satan is that the group exists for the same purpose the Illuminati does--to create and maintain one central global authoritarian government under the rule of communism. In fact, the Synagogue of Satan is, in Carr's eyes, made up of the same people who comprise the Illuminati. In Carr's theory, however, the group has actually existed for a very long time (before even the life of Jesus Christ and the beginnings of Christianity). This is a markedly different approach to the historicity of the New World Order than others have taken; most theorists begin their histories in modern times (at the earliest with the French Revolution).

William Guy Carr's theories are pivotal to any understanding of the Illuminati as they stand in the modern world. While there is no way to prove the validity of Carr's theories, it is also impossible to ever truly disprove them--nothing has been heard of from the Order of Illuminati since 1785, and thus there is both a chance that they dispersed completely at this point and a chance that the group continued its work even more underground than it ever had before, as Carr and others believe.

Carr's theories of the Three World Wars and the Synagogue of Satan are also important in how pervasive they have become in the conspiracy community. His theories also prove just how important John Robison and Augustin Barruel's own theories have become--in publicly critiquing the Illuminati for an English-speaking audience, Robison and Barruel created a narrative of the Illuminati which is still popular, widely believed, and has inspired many other theories through modern times.

The Illuminati and Pop Culture

Beyond the in-depth theories which have been published in the latter half of the 20th century, the Illuminati has also taken on a life of its own within the realm of pop culture. It has always been supposed that the members of the über-underground version of the Illuminati are powerful, in elite standing within society, and, most importantly, hold the power to influence the general public at every whim.

For this reason, the most recent wave of Illuminati conspiracies revolve around pop culture icons, especially those in the music and film industries. These icons have the power to reach mass amounts of people at the snap of their fingers, and thus are in an ideal position to be carrying out the Illuminati's goals of world domination.

One of the main speculations about Illuminati leaders as they exist today centers on Beyoncé and Jay-Z. References to the Illuminati and other secret societies have been popular in rap and R&B lyrics since the 1990s, but Jay-Z furthered these references through the use of his signature hand symbol: holding up both palms so the thumbs and index fingers form a triangle.

While this hand symbol may at first seem innocuous, theorists say that the triangle has a direct relationship to the pyramid shape, a symbol which features prominently in Illuminati theories. The pyramid, in

Illuminati theories, often represents the top-down command structure of the secret society. The top of the pyramid represents the "one percent," those who hold ultimate power in the organization, with the bottom layers representing the general public.

The pyramid actually has links which reach back to the original Order of Illuminati in Bavaria, as well. Pyramids were reportedly used as decoration at meetings of the Order, especially on carpets, which often featured a pyramid with the letters "D" and "P" on either side of it, standing for Deo Proximo--God is Near.

Unfinished pyramids also featured prominently in the Order of Illuminati, signifying that the Order's work of building a perfect world was consistently incomplete. By working together, the Illuminati could work to finish their pyramid, the New World Order. An unfinished pyramid was often used in Freemason literature as well.

Jay-Z's use of the triangle as a hand symbol during his concerts sparked rumors that he was, indeed, one of the leaders of the Illuminati. In 2010, Jay-Z addressed these rumors in a song called "Free Mason," where he says: "I said I was amazing, not that I'm a Mason / . . . I'm red hot, I'm on my third six, but a devil I'm not." This did not quell the stories and theories--instead, it seemed to add fuel to the fire, with fans soon questioning every minute detail of Jay-Z's tracks and videos for clues about his involvement.

When Beyoncé and Jay-Z's daughter was born in 2012, theorists began wondering if the Illuminati couple's daughter had anything to do with the organization's goals. They speculated that their daughter's name, Blue Ivy, was actually a complicated Illuminati acronym, with each letter standing for a word: Born Living Under Evil, Ilumianti's Very Youngest. Internet publications also theorized that Blue Ivy's name, when spoken in reverse, was eerily similar to the Latin name for Lucifer's daughter. Theorists feared that the birth of Blue Ivy was a sign of Beyoncé and Jay-Z's ultimate alliances.

The following year, Beyoncé performed at the Super Bowl halftime show, one of the most-watched television events in history.

During the performance--watched live by nearly 100 million people--Beyoncé held up the same hand symbol for which her husband had become known: the finger triangle. Then, during the third quarter of the football game, more than half of the lights went out in the stadium where the Superbowl was being held. Theories blew up across the internet--what kind of power did Beyoncé truly possess?

From 2013 forward, conspiracy theorists picked apart just about every one of Beyoncé and Jay-Z's videos and songs for evidence of Illuminati allegiances. Much of these analyses rest the weight of their arguments on what is thought to be Illuminati symbolism--for example, Beyoncé was once photographed wearing a ring depicting a goat, which was thought to be a tribute to Baphomet, a pagan deity to whom the Illuminati are thought to have aligned themselves with.

While each of these mini-theories (often posted to YouTube or fan discussion boards) only brings with it only a small thread of evidence, believers of the theories see them all fitting together into a larger picture of Illuminati elites.

One example of a popular Beyoncé Illuminati theory which appeared during this time is that her 2009 video for "Crazy in Love" is actually a thinly coded, step-by-step depiction of her initiation into the Illuminati. It is in this video that Beyoncé's alter ego, Sasha Fierce, is born, and it is theorized that this rebirth is actually how she was initiated into the Illuminati. In the video, it is theorized, Beyoncé is shown selling her soul for fame and fortune, and, at the video's conclusion, Beyoncé is blown up while sitting in a car. Afterward, Beyoncé's alter ego appears next to Jay-Z, and he refers to her as "Young B," because she has just been reborn as the Illuminati version of herself.

In 2016, Beyoncé surprise dropped the "Formation" video online, and its coded language and myriad of references to black life in America stirred up quite a bit of hate speech. In the video, Beyoncé takes a stand against those who say she is the leader of a conspiracy, just as Jay-Z did many years earlier (albeit in an even more outright manner), beginning the song "Y'all haters corny with that Illuminati mess."

Theorists went wild at this very direct statement--but it was not at all surprising to them, and, in fact, theorists said that denial is exactly how elite members of the Illuminati have always reacted.

While Beyoncé and Jay-Z have certainly stirred up the most Illuminati-connected theories in recent years, other high-ranking pop culture icons have been theorized about as well. Kanye West, Kim Kardashian, Lindsay Lohan, Lebron James, Rihanna, and Lady Gaga have all had theories written about their connections to the Illuminati, most again backed by photographic evidence of Illuminati symbols (such as the triangle or the "666" hand symbol).

While theories about the Illuminati's whereabouts and membership have always had a place in whispered conferences and shadowy publications since the 18th century, the rise of the internet and popular culture has allowed these theories a full-bodied voice in contemporary society.

Conclusion

By all accounts and documentation, the Illuminati did at some point in time exist in a solid way. The Order of Illuminati began as just five men with a vision of changing the world, and, while the original organization was only officially in existence for nine years, it spawned generations upon generations of wonder at the inner workings of the world.

Adam Weishaupt, Bavarian rationalist, began the Order of Illuminati in 1776, and from its very birth the organization gave rise to questions about its true intentions. When work is done in the shadows, there will always be those who would like to hold it up to the light, and this was certainly true in the case of the Illuminati. Sure, they were hoping to make change in the world--but what kind of change were the Illuminati truly after, if they had to work in secret to motivate it?

For the English-speaking world, the Illuminati's storied and secretive past was, for the most part, narrated by those who saw the organization as a dangerous one--John Robison and Augustin Barruel in particular viewed the Illuminati as an imminent threat to Bavarian society and the world at large. Robison and Barruel were also responsible, in their own respects, for fueling the first large-scale conspiracy theory about the Illuminati: that the group had fomented and were responsible for the French Revolution.

From this point on, the Illuminati's reputation was consistently one wrapped up with fear of an unknown power. If the group could exist without leaving any trace of their activities, it was also possible that the Illuminati had the power to pull strings in all areas of society.

The truly terrifying aspect of the Illuminati became the fact that it could not be proven to exist, at least by any hard or official evidence--it exists just beyond the reach of our collective peripheral vision, just beyond our grasp, and, while we cannot fully take hold of or comprehend the Illuminati's activities, it can continue to exist, enacting its powerful legacy upon the world.

Many people disregard theories about the modern Illuminati as rantings and ravings of people who are far too suspicious, or of those who should be more trusting of those with societal influence, while others buy into the theories with no questions asked, looking around every corner for the beast lurking in the shadows.

While the stories about the Illuminati's underground doings lost some steam from the mid-1800s to the end of World War I, they found a place again in post-war America, in a society which felt enemies and oppressors breathing down its neck at every junction. Theories about the Illuminati found a new home in the United States, where their figured loomed larger and more menacing than ever before.

Today, the Illuminati has become a legacy of suspicions and conspiracies, a shadow of the organization which planted its roots in Bavaria so many years ago--albeit a shadow which seems to grow larger every day. The Illuminati went from a humble society of men looking to rationalize the world and enact good to a worldwide underground network with far loftier and nefarious aims: total world domination.

Popular culture and access to the internet has breathed new life into theories about the whereabouts of the Illuminati. More people than ever before have the name of the secret society on their lips, and, while many of these people do not believe the stories they hear, it is important nonetheless that the group's legacy lives on. The Illuminati began its life in secret, and, as far as we know, they could continue to act in secret today. These theories are no more provable than they were 200 years ago, but they have not yet ceased to perplex and amaze us and, it seems, they will continue to do so into the foreseeable future.

Printed in Great Britain
by Amazon